SUMMARY of Jason Fung's THE OBESITY CODE

Unlocking the Secrets of Weight Loss

by SUMOREADS

Copyright © 2017 by SUMOREADS. All rights reserved. This book or parts thereof may not be reproduced in any form, stored in any retrieval system, or transmitted in any form by any means—electronic, mechanical, photocopy, recording, or otherwise—without prior written permission of the publisher, except as provided by United States of America copyright law. This is an unofficial summary and is not intended as a substitute or replacement for the original book.

TABLE OF CONTENTS

EXECUTIVE SUMMARY 6

PART ONE: THE EPIDEMIC 7
Key Takeaway: Calories are the proximate, not the ultimate, cause of obesity
Key Takeaway: Scientifically flawed advice underlies the ballooning of the obesity epidemic
Key Takeaway: Obesity is mostly inherited

PART TWO: THE CALORIE DECEPTION 9
Key Takeaway: Obesity is not a caloric disorder
Key Takeaway: The human body is coded for efficiency and self-preservation
Key Takeaway: Exercise has a negligible effect on weight loss
Key Takeaway: Over- and underfeeding have negligible long-term effects on weight
Key Takeaway: Obesity stems from an imbalance in the hormones that regulate fat growth

PART THREE: A NEW MODEL OF OBESITY 13
Key Takeaway: Insulin directs fat accumulation and storage.
Key Takeaway: High levels of insulin cause obesity
Key Takeaway: Excessive secretion of cortisol causes weight gain
Key Takeaway: The low-carb Atkins diet was unsustainable because it was incomplete
Key Takeaway: High carbohydrate intake does not necessarily increase insulin
Key Takeaway: Excessive insulin creates insulin resistance, which creates a vicious cycle

Key Takeaway: Insulin levels and resistance rise and fall on meal composition and timing

PART FOUR: THE SOCIAL PHENOMENON OF OBESITY 18

Key Takeaway: Snacking is an elaborate Big Food deception
Key Takeaway: Skip breakfast—it's only important for companies selling breakfast
Key Takeaway: Obesity is largely a creation of government policy
Key Takeaway: Insulin causes obesity across all age brackets.

PART FIVE: WHAT'S WRONG WITH OUR DIET? ..21

Key Takeaway: Fructose builds insulin resistance
Key Takeaway: Eliminate added sugars from your diet to avoid weight gain
Key Takeaway: The weight-gain effect of carbohydrates depends on their processing
Key Takeaway: Processing removes the food components that naturally limit insulin levels
Key Takeaway: It's not just carbohydrates that raise insulin levels
Key Takeaway: There is no link between dietary fat and cardiovascular disease, or obesity.

PART SIX: THE SOLUTION 25

Key Takeaway: Diets fail because they ignore the multifactorial nature of human disease
Key Takeaway: An effective weight-reduction plan targets the cause of high insulin levels
Key Takeaway: Cut back consumption of added sugars to reduce insulin spikes
Key Takeaway: Avoid all snacks to keep insulin levels stable
Key Takeaway: Skip breakfast if you are not hungry

Key Takeaway: Decrease consumption of refined grains to improve your weight-loss potential

Key Takeaway: Consume moderate amounts of proteins and increase natural fats

Key Takeaway: Eat more dietary fiber to moderate insulin and weight gain

Key Takeaway: Intermittent fasting is the second half of the weight-loss equation

Key Takeaway: Go on regular, short-period fasts to lower insulin levels and cut weight

Key Takeaway: Exercise and meditative practice reduce cortisol and lower insulin levels

EDITORIAL REVIEW 30

ABOUT THE AUTHOR..32

EXECUTIVE SUMMARY

In his book *The Obesity Code: Unlocking the Secrets of Weight Loss*, Jason Fung chronicles the ballooning of the obesity epidemic from the 1970s to date and proposes a hormonal theory of obesity that sheds light on obesity as a hormonal imbalance disorder rather than a caloric imbalance disorder.

He argues that conventional advice to eat less and move more fails because it ignores the multifactorial nature of obesity, and because the body has an efficient homeostatic mechanism that moderates changes in caloric intake and expenditure to maintain a set weight. In his view, obesity is a multifactorial disease with carbohydrates, calories, sugar, and insulin resistance converging to create the hormonal imbalances that lead to weight gain. He identifies excessive insulin, which is stimulated by persistently high levels of glucose, as the ultimate cause of obesity.

Fung contends that dieters fail because they regard meal portions and exercise routines with hawk-eyed scrutiny while the real culprits of obesity—meal content and timing—go unaddressed. He proposes a combination of a diet low on sugar and processed foods and intermittent fasting to limit insulin spikes, reduce insulin levels and, consequently, lower weight.

PART ONE: THE EPIDEMIC

Key Takeaway: Calories are the proximate, not the ultimate, cause of obesity

Every human condition has a proximate and an ultimate cause, the effective management of which depends on the understanding of both. The proximate or immediate cause of alcoholism, for example, is excessive intake of alcohol. The ultimate cause—the one that led to excessive intake of alcohol—may be stress, an addictive personality, or even the addictive nature of alcohol itself. Mediation efforts that singularly focus on the proximate cause are a fool's errand.

It's plausible that the immediate cause of weight gain is the consumption of more calories than the body expends. The ultimate cause of obesity, however, is multifactorial. Obesity is a product of hormonal imbalance, among other things. Conventional advice to eat less and move more doesn't work because it ignores the root causes of obesity.

Key Takeaway: Scientifically flawed advice underlies the ballooning of the obesity epidemic

In 1977, the United States' Committee on Nutrition and Human Needs issued a report titled *Dietary Goals for the United States* to settle the long-standing dietary debate. The report recommended the consumption of less fat and more carbohydrates. In the years that followed, the consumption of refined carbohydrates and sugar increased, and fat intake decreased.

The implications of the report would manifest decades later. Between the 1970s and early 2000s, the percentage of obese adults in the United States increased from about 15 percent to a staggering 40 percent.

Key Takeaway: Obesity is mostly inherited

In a study of 540 Danish adult adoptees, Dr. Albert J. Stunkard found that there was no relationship between the weight of the adoptees and their adoptive parents. Remarkably, the weight of the adoptees had a strong and consistent relationship with that of their biological parents—who had nothing to do with their dietary or exercise choices. In another study of identical and fraternal twins who grew up in separate homes, Dr. Stunkard found that genes accounted for approximately 70 percent of the subject's tendency to gain weight.

These findings discounted the role of the environmental factors thought to cause obesity—mostly dietary habits and lack of exercise. However, the dramatic increase in the prevalence of obesity from the 1970s indicates that genetics is not the only contributing factor.

PART TWO: THE CALORIE DECEPTION

Key Takeaway: Obesity is not a caloric disorder

The proposition that body fat is the product of consuming more calories than expended is a fallacy. It erroneously assumes that:

• All calories have the same weight-gain effect, yet calories from different foods elicit different metabolic and hormonal responses.

• Calories expended are independent of the calories consumed. They are dependent. If you reduce 30 percent of the calories you consume, your body will expend 30 percent less calories.

• Eating too much is a conscious choice. Hormones that signal hunger and satiety play a major role in what and how much you eat.

• Only exercise has a significant effect on caloric expenditure—the body expends any excess energy in added heat, increased heart rate, new tissue production, excretion, and numerous other ways, depending on many factors. Exercise only accounts for about 5 percent of total energy expenditure.

Caloric intake in the United States remained virtually unchanged between 1990 and 2010. Yet, in these two decades, obesity increased by about 0.37 percent every year.

"The low-fat, low-calorie diet has already been proven to fail. This is the cruel hoax. Eating less does not result in lasting weight loss" (p. 47).

Key Takeaway: The human body is coded for efficiency and self-preservation

Calorie-reduction dieting doesn't work for the simple reason that the body is built to be ruthlessly efficient.

When you reduce caloric intake, your body automatically reduces your metabolic rate—your heart rate, new tissue growth, brain function, body temperature, and all other body functions that require energy—to even out the deficit and preserve itself. These energy expenditure cuts not only cause the lethargy you feel when you diet, but they also limit weight loss.

When you stop dieting, the low metabolic rate persists, meaning your calorie intake vastly exceeds your calorie expenditure. This imbalance is what causes rapid weight gain after dieting.

Key Takeaway: Exercise has a negligible effect on weight loss

The human body expends most of its energy not through exercise, but through housekeeping tasks such as breathing, pumping blood, maintaining body temperature, and maintaining brain and other vital functions. Some of the energy is used in non-exercise activities like cooking and walking.

Exercise is ineffective for weight loss because of two compensation mechanisms: increasing calorie expenditure elicits an urge to eat more to fill the deficit, and increasing exercise decreases non-exercise activity so that the body doesn't over-exert itself. In separate studies, women who did aerobics six days a week for a year lost an average of three pounds, and sedentary men who trained to run a marathon only lost five pounds.

Key Takeaway: Over- and underfeeding have negligible long-term effects on weight

Overeating is largely a myth because it's impossible to eat past a certain point. Even when you overeat, the body increases metabolism to expend the excess energy. Increased body heat, for example, may expend up to 70 percent of the excess energy.

The weight you gain when you overfeed is, ultimately, a fraction of what the calorie theory predicts. You don't retain this weight for long, just as you can't hold off for long the weight you lose by underfeeding. Internal physiological sensors adjust metabolism to return body weight and fat to its set point, to its stable equilibrium. For obese people, this set point is just too high.

Key Takeaway: Obesity stems from an imbalance in the hormones that regulate fat growth

Everything in your body—from your growth and sexual maturation to your blood sugar and body temperature—is regulated by hormones. The hormones that regulate fat growth—including leptin, adiponectin, and lipase—are at the core of the development of obesity.

Leptin—a protein produced by fat cells—travels through the blood to the hypothalamus. Based on the amount of leptin it receives, the hypothalamus tells the body to reduce or increase appetite or metabolism to maintain fat stores at the set point. If fat mass decreases, for example, leptin levels fall and the hypothalamus stimulates appetite. If no food is ingested, it sends signals to lower metabolism and limit energy expenditure.

In this way, the hypothalamus, through the input of leptin, regulates energy balance and, consequently, body weight.

Damage to the hypothalamus has been known to lead to uncontrollable weight gain, even when patients are on a near-starvation diet.

PART THREE:
A NEW MODEL OF OBESITY

Key Takeaway: Insulin directs fat accumulation and storage

Insulin is the key that unlocks cells so that they can absorb glucose from the bloodstream and use it for energy. It also tells cells to store some of the glucose in the liver for later use (when glucose levels fall) and the excess as fat for much later use (when the glycogen stored in the liver is exhausted). The amount of glucose in the blood depends on the food you eat. Protein and dietary fats have minimal effects on blood sugar levels. Refined carbohydrates—which are basically sugar—raise blood sugar and, consequently, stimulate the release of insulin.

If you eat frequently—and, consequently, maintain your glycogen storage—the body has no need to burn fat, so it accumulates. In a normal balance, high levels of insulin stimulate the body to store sugar and fat, and low levels stimulate it to burn glycogen and fat. When you balance periods of eating and fasting, the body does not gain or lose any fat.

Key Takeaway: High levels of insulin cause obesity

Compared to lean people, obese people secrete very high levels of insulin when they eat, and these levels remain relatively high even after the meal. High levels of insulin increase fat storage and raise the body set weight. When the body set weight increases, the hypothalamus sends hunger and appetite signals and, in the absence of food, induces lowered metabolism to take the body to the new set weight.

"As the insightful Gary Taubes wrote in his book Why We Get Fat: And What to Do about It, *'We do not get fat because we overeat. We overeat because we get fat'"* (p. 86).

Long-term studies have shown that drugs that introduce insulin into the body, increase insulin sensitivity, or stimulate the pancreas to produce more insulin cause significant gains in weight regardless of caloric intake. Conditions or drugs that reduce insulin levels in the body have an opposite effect. One of the defining characteristic of type 1 diabetes—a disease that destroys insulin-producing cells in the pancreas—is severe weight loss, regardless of the number of calories the patient consumes.

Key Takeaway: Excessive secretion of cortisol causes weight gain

The stress hormone cortisol activates the fight-or-flight mechanism by temporarily restricting metabolic functions and moving glucose and glycogen to muscles to provide energy to fight or flee. When you face a physical threat, your body burns the glucose made available as you fight or flee. Chronic stress raises glucose levels indefinitely because there is no physical exertion to burn the glucose made available.

By enhancing glucose levels, cortisol triggers an increase in insulin levels, and high insulin levels stimulate fat storage and cause weight gain. Damage to the adrenal gland, which produces cortisol, causes weight loss in up to 97 percent of patients.

Sleep deprivation—one of the leading causes of chronic stress—stimulates cortisol and decreases insulin sensitivity. By so doing, it dramatically increases the risk of weight gain, especially for people who sleep less than seven hours a night.

Key Takeaway: The low-carb Atkins diet was unsustainable because it was incomplete

In the early 1960s, Dr. Robert Atkins argued that highly refined carbohydrates raise blood sugar, which raises insulin levels, which causes obesity.

In recent years, studies have proved that Atkins' low-carb diet is better at improving cholesterol, blood sugar, and blood pressure and lowering body weight than low-fat diets like the Ornish and Zone diet. The Atkins diet works, at least in the short-term, because it reduces insulin levels, maintains metabolism, and reduces appetite.

However, most Atkins dieters regain weight after about a year because low-carb compliance is difficult and because the proteins the diet champions also raise insulin levels, which cause weight gain. Additionally, the diet does not make provisions for fasting to break constant levels of insulin and achieve long-term weight loss.

Key Takeaway: High carbohydrate intake does not necessarily increase insulin

Dr. Atkins' hypothesis was incomplete in that it failed to mention that sugar intake made a larger contribution to obesity than carbohydrates, and that refined and whole carbohydrates have different effects on insulin levels.

Instances of obesity among Asians, for example, have been rare until recently, even though white rice has been their staple food for nearly fifty years. The reason for this paradox, according to an Intermap study, is low sucrose consumption, which minimizes insulin simulation and insulin resistance. In primitive societies who consume diets rich in unrefined carbohydrates, virtually all people have low insulin levels and normal BMIs.

Key Takeaway: Excessive insulin creates insulin resistance, which creates a vicious cycle

Long-term obesity is a self-driving condition that becomes harder to treat over time. High levels of insulin create insulin resistance, which stimulates even higher levels of insulin regardless of the diet. This vicious cycle balloons upwards over time and makes the obese more obese.

Insulin is the key that opens the receptor that lets glucose molecules into cells. Insulin resistance develops when the receptors are exposed to persistently high levels of insulin, much like antibiotic resistance develops from high doses of antibiotics. At the onset of insulin resistance, fewer glucose molecules enter cells, so the body increases insulin levels to open more receptors and let the original amount of glucose in. Insulin resistance is the body's way of protecting itself—very high levels of insulin would elicit the extraction of too much glucose from the bloodstream and cause seizures and, ultimately, death.

Key Takeaway: Insulin levels and resistance rise and fall on meal composition and timing

Hormonal resistance develops in response to constant stimulus and high and persistent levels of hormones. If insulin levels are low most of the time, or if spikes are only periodic, the body does not develop resistance. Essentially, what you eat, and when you eat it, determines whether or not you develop insulin resistance.

Timing is the vital half of dieting. Three meals a day, spread at, say, breakfast at 8 a.m., lunch at noon and dinner at 6 p.m., balance a few hours of insulin spikes with several hours of low insulin levels. When you increase eating opportunities by snacking between meals, you expose your body to constant and persistently high levels of insulin. It's no surprise that the increase of daily meals from three to six between the 1960s and 2014 coincided with an increase in obesity.

PART FOUR: THE SOCIAL PHENOMENON OF OBESITY

Key Takeaway: Snacking is an elaborate Big Food deception

Eating more often to lose weight is as absurd as it sounds. Yet it has become popular diet advice, peddled by big food companies and the health, nutritional, and research organizations they sponsor, because eating more means more profits. Snacking may reduce the calories you consume in the subsequent meal, but the calorie reduction won't be big enough to cancel out the calories in the snack itself.

Key Takeaway: Skip breakfast—it's only important for companies selling breakfast

The idea that breakfast is the most important meal of the day is a dysfunctional North American belief. A heavy breakfast does not reduce the amount of food you eat throughout the day, and it certainly does not contribute to weight loss. Most people in France, where the population has predominantly normal BMIs, only take coffee for breakfast.

The moment you wake up, a mix of cortisol, growth hormone, and adrenaline automatically stimulates your liver to make glucose to power your morning. Morning hunger, if it exists, is only a learned behavior. Breakfast has virtually no effect on your energy levels.

Key Takeaway: Obesity is largely a creation of government policy

Statistics from the Center for Disease Control reveal a strong correlation between poverty and obesity. Mississippi, the poorest state in the U.S., has the highest level of obesity. Affluent states, which have relatively low rates of obesity, pose a paradox because the people in these states have occupations that require minimal physical exertion and can afford to be indulgent.

Refined carbohydrates, and the government policies that promote their production and consumption, explain obesity in poor states. Since dietary fats are not very palatable, and since dietary proteins are relatively expensive, most people living in poverty are left to eat processed carbohydrates, which are plentiful and inexpensive. Part of the reason processed carbohydrates are cheap is because foods like corn, wheat, and soybeans as well as food additives like corn syrup and soy oils get the largest share of government subsidies. High subsidies encourage large-scale production of these foods, make them cheaper, and, consequently, encourage their consumption.

Key Takeaway: Insulin causes obesity across all age brackets

The overfeeding and under-exercising theory of obesity is not only evidence-deficient; it also fails to explain why the prevalence of obesity among children between zero and six months is on the rise.

Excessive insulin explains the prevalence of obesity across the board, especially among children. When a mother has high insulin levels, she passes these hormonal imbalances to her fetus through the placenta, and the cycle of high insulin continues as the fetus develops insulin resistance. An obese mother is likely to give birth to an obese child, and an obese child is up to seventeen times more likely to grow into an obese adult, who will give birth to an obese child.

PART FIVE: WHAT'S WRONG WITH OUR DIET?

Key Takeaway: Fructose builds insulin resistance

The consumption of sugar-sweetened drinks, including sodas and sweetened tea and juices, has grown tremendously since the 1970s—as has the prevalence of obesity. Only recently has consumption declined amid health concerns and political opposition. Daily consumption of sugary drinks and fructose (high-fructose corn syrup is a popular ingredient in processed foods, including breads, ketchup, and sauces) not only poses the risk of substantial weight gain, but also multiplies the risk of developing type 2 diabetes.

Unlike glucose, which can be used by every cell in the body, fructose is only processed by the liver and cannot be used for energy. Some of the end products of fructose build up in liver cells, damaging liver function and causing insulin resistance. In a 2009 study, healthy subjects consuming excessive amounts of fructose developed insulin resistance in just six days and pre-diabetes in eight weeks.

Key Takeaway: Eliminate added sugars from your diet to avoid weight gain

Foods or drinks with fructose are the obvious candidates for elimination. Remove all sweetened drinks, including sodas, sugar-added juices and teas, and other soft drinks from your diet.

Drinks with artificial sweeteners are equally deceptive. Studies not sponsored by food companies have consistently shown that substituting sugar with artificial sweeteners has no beneficial effect on weight.

Although diet drinks have few calories and no sugar, they raise insulin levels and, consequently, increase the risk of obesity by almost 50 percent over a decade. Two or more diet sodas consumed every day also raise the risk of strokes and heart attacks considerably.

Key Takeaway: The weight-gain effect of carbohydrates depends on their processing

The glycemic index indicates how much foods raise blood glucose levels and assigns them a value. Fats and proteins have an insignificant effect on blood glucose, so they are excluded from the index. The glycemic load accounts for serving size to accommodate the fact that 50-gram servings of different foods have varying amounts of carbohydrates.

Despite having the same carbohydrate content, processed foods like cornflakes, cheerios, and white bread have high glycemic indexes and load scores, and traditional whole foods, like boiled potatoes, bananas, and brown rice, have low glycemic scores. Processing purifies and concentrates carbohydrates and, consequently, increases their glycemic scores. When wheat is milled into fine flour, more of the glucose in it is absorbed faster in the bloodstream than if it were consumed as whole grain.

Key Takeaway: Processing removes the food components that naturally limit insulin levels

Processing removes most dietary fibers, fats, and proteins to increase the taste, texture, and durability of food. By so doing, it wrecks the natural balances that help keep insulin levels in check.

Fiber, for example, is the non-digestible part of carbohydrates that fills the stomach, reduces food intake, and decreases absorption and digestion. By decreasing absorption of carbohydrates, fiber reduces both blood glucose and insulin levels. Nearly all unrefined plant foods have fiber. This explains why traditional societies ate carbohydrate-dense natural foods but had rare cases of obesity.

Key Takeaway: It's not just carbohydrates that raise insulin levels

The glycemic index misleads weight watchers because it considers foods that raise blood glucose, not insulin levels. Insulin levels can rise even in the absence of glucose, and blood glucose only accounts for about a quarter of the insulin stimulated. The insulin index, which measures how much insulin levels rise in response to ingested food, is a better indicator of the fattening effect of foods, especially for the fats and proteins ignored by the glycemic index.

When food is in the mouth, the body anticipates it and—regardless of what food it is—increases insulin levels. In this sense, any food can cause weight gain. Fats and proteins account for 10 percent of the insulin secreted. Close to 70 percent of the insulin secreted has no known stimulant.

"There are no intrinsically bad foods, only processed ones. The further you stray from real food, the more danger you are in... Should you eat processed meats, processed fats or processed carbohydrates? No, no and no" (p. 200).

Key Takeaway: There is no link between dietary fat and cardiovascular disease, or obesity.

Cholesterol is an organic molecule found in abundance in the body. The liver manufactures as much as 80 percent of blood cholesterol to be used to buildthe membranes that surround cells. The 1950s studies that popularized the idea that high blood cholesterol levels cause heart disease were nothing more than correlation studies. Later studies have shown that the intake of saturated fats does not increase blood cholesterol or cause heart disease.

Most nutrition advice is flawed because it reduces foods to generalized absurdities. Champions of low-fat diets, for example, assume all fats are the same, but anyone can guess that an avocado and a teaspoon of margarine, which have the same fat content, have vastly different nutritional values. While artificial trans fats such as margarine increase bad cholesterol, lower good cholesterol, and increase the risk of heart disease, natural saturated fats such as butter reduce the risk of heart attack. Taken with other foods, cheese, sour cream, whole milk, and other sources of dietary fat lessen glucose and insulin spikes.

PART SIX: THE SOLUTION

Key Takeaway: Diets fail because they ignore the multifactorial nature of human disease

All diets—be it the Mediterranean diet, the low-fat low calorie diet, or the Atkins diet—are similar in one way: they lead to weight loss, but only in the short term. Progress plateaus in six to twelve months, and the weight lost comes back afterward despite strict adherence to the diet's guidelines.

At first, diets work because they address one or two of the factors that cause weight gain and trick the hypothalamus to lower the body set weight. But when the set weight declines, the body fights back to restore the equilibrium.

Key Takeaway: An effective weight-reduction plan targets the cause of high insulin levels

Since obesity is a multifactorial disease—with carbs, calories, sugars, proteins, fats, and sleep deprivation contributing to its prognosis—a diet that addresses one or two factors and ignores the others is not sustainable.

An obesity management program has to start with an assessment of the cause of the hormonal imbalance at the root of the condition. If the cause of high insulin levels is excessive consumption of sugar or carbohydrates, cutting back on these foods would be the logical place to start. If it's chronic sleep deprivation, that should be the first thing to address.

Key Takeaway: Cut back consumption of added sugars to reduce insulin spikes

To kick start your weight loss plan, start by eliminating table sugar from your food or beverages. Eliminate artificial sweeteners as well because they raise insulin levels as much as sugar does.

Almost all processed foods have added sugars. Names like glucose, sucrose, fructose, corn sweetener, maltose, and nectar, which food companies use on food labels, are all sugar pseudonyms. Sauces and commercial condiments such as ketchup have large amounts of sugar and should wisely be reduced.

Sweetened drinks, including vitamin water, fruit juice, smoothies, iced coffee, and energy drinks, have a lot of added sugars. When it comes to beverages, plain or sparkling water—with an optional slice of lemon or cucumber—is your best bet. Moderate amounts of red wine—up to two glasses a day—have beneficial health effects and can safely be added to a diet.

Replace desserts such as cakes, candy, puddings, and ice cream with nuts, cheeses, fresh fruits, or moderate amounts of dark chocolate.

Key Takeaway: Avoid all snacks to keep insulin levels stable

If you are like most people, you snack when you are bored, not when you are hungry. Snacking keeps insulin levels constantly elevated and, consequently, builds insulin resistance over time. Most snacks cause immediate insulin spikes because they contain high amounts of refined flour and sugar. A cup of green tea is a good replacement for snacks.

Key Takeaway: Skip breakfast if you are not hungry

If you listen to your body, you will find that you are not really hungry in the morning. You can take coffee, tea, or water when you wake up and have your first meal at noon.

Most breakfast options contain a lot of refined carbohydrates and sugars. Replace bakery products, instant oatmeal, and sugared breakfast cereals with whole, unprocessed foods such as eggs.

Key Takeaway: Decrease consumption of refined grains to improve your weight-loss potential

Refined grains such as white flour are not only low on nutrients, but they also stimulate insulin more than other foods. Reduce the consumption of white flour, bakery foods, pasta and noodles to a minimum to curtail insulin spikes and increase your weight-loss potential. Whole grains and other unprocessed carbohydrates are ideal choices because they have the fiber that prevents insulin surges.

Key Takeaway: Consume moderate amounts of proteins and increase natural fats

Proteins should account for a maximum of between 20 and 30 percent of your total calories.

Dietary fats are less likely to stimulate insulin than carbohydrates and proteins. Whereas highly processed vegetable oils—including "pure olive oil"—may contribute to the risk of heart disease, natural, unprocessed fats such as butter, coconut oil, and virgin olive oil have antioxidant and anti-inflammatory benefits that lower cholesterol and the risk of cardiovascular disease. Full-fat dairy will have virtually no effect on your weight.

Key Takeaway: Eat more dietary fiber to moderate insulin and weight gain

Studies have demonstrated that the dietary fiber in natural whole foods has weight-lowering effects—as does vinegar, which lessens insulin spikes.

Key Takeaway: Intermittent fasting is the second half of the weight-loss equation

It's not enough to watch the foods you eat; you must watch *when* you eat. Increasing the time you take meals will keep insulin levels elevated and cause more weight gain than increasing your food portions.

Since insulin resistance develops from persistently high insulin levels, it can only be broken by repeat periods of very low insulin levels. Eating the right foods only prevents insulin spikes. What lowers insulin levels is fasting—precisely intermittent fasts of twenty-four to thirty-six hours.

Twenty four hours into a fast, glucose is depleted, insulin levels fall, and the body begins to process the glycogen stored in the liver to provide energy. Between one to three days into the fast, fat is broken into fatty acids to provide energy to maintain tissues. Concerns over malnutrition, hunger spells, and muscle-wasting during fasting are unfounded because the body is well adapted to cope with a transitory absence of food. Total energy expenditure actually increases over a fast, and adrenaline increases to maintain energy levels.

Diets fail because they are constants—the body acclimates to the cuts and adjusts its internal mechanisms to revert to its original weight. Fasting works because of its intermittent nature. It has been a part of culture for millennia—anyone can do it.

"These are times to celebrate and indulge. But there is also a time to fast. We cannot change this cycle of life. We cannot feast all the time. We cannot fast all the time. It won't work. It doesn't work" (p. 248).

Key Takeaway: Go on regular, short-period fasts to lower insulin levels and cut weight

Fasting means keeping off all foods and drinks. The only exceptions are drinks with no calories such as water and tea—which are vital to hydration—and broths. Bone and vegetable broths (homemade, not the canned varieties) are also good for fasting days. Take some salt in your drinks or broths to keep minerals in your bloodstream and prevent muscle cramping.

The recommended fasting periods are twelve to thirty-six hours, two or three times a week. For a twenty-hour fast, skip two consecutive meals and take one meal of choice. For a thirty-six hour fast, skip three consecutive meals. If you feel hungry, keep yourself busy, take some water or other non-caloric drink and it will pass. Break your fast with light meals and take healthy and normal food portions afterwards. You can do any type of exercise as you fast—your liver and fat stores will supply the energy you need.

Key Takeaway: Exercise and meditative practice reduce cortisol and lower insulin levels

Chronic stress raises cortisol levels, which raise insulin levels, which cause obesity. If stress is the cause of your weight gain, minimize your exposure to stressful situations as much as you can, increase your social connectedness, and take on an active practice—exercise, yoga, meditation, or massage—to lower your cortisol levels.

EDITORIAL REVIEW

In his book *The Obesity Code,* Jason Fung argues that excessive secretion of insulin, not overeating or being sedentary, is the ultimate cause of obesity. Insulin instructs cells to extract glucose from the bloodstream, use some as energy, and store the rest as glycogen and fat. Excessive insulin—which is stimulated by processed grains and sugars and continuous ingestion—directs the body to store more fat and hold on to its fat reserves. The only way to moderate insulin levels and lower weight, he contends, is to minimize the consumption of refined carbs and sugars and go on short, periodic fasts.

What Fung offers is not new weight-loss advice. Recommendations to reduce dietary sugar and refined grains, increase fiber and natural fats, and go on fasts have been around long before obesity became a mainstream concern. By his admission, fasting has been a spiritual practice for millennia. What Fung offers is a robust "why": Why eat unprocessed and not refined grains, why cut back on sugars, and why go on intermittent fasts. He goes out of his way to answer these *whys* and, by so doing, makes his weight-loss recommendations palatable.

Fung takes near-constant jabs at the caloric theory of obesity which argues that fat is accumulated when the calories consumed exceed the calories expended. He devotes entire chapters to unraveling what he calls a "calorie deception" and argues that the body always adjusts its metabolism to even out caloric cuts or additions and retain its set weight. Perhaps because of this overemphasis on the *other* argument, part of his writing comes off as skewed, incomplete even. He fails to mention, for example, why his readers should limit protein intake to between the 20 and 30 percent of total calories he recommends. Without a rationale, this recommendation sounds as arbitrary as the dieting advice he so much castigates.

All the same, Fung redeems himself with the simple analogies and hundreds of scientific studies he uses to illustrate and support his argument. Extensive research makes *The Obesity Code* a time machine to back when Western countries became fat nations, an extensive exploration of the hormonal human body, an exposé of the pervasive myths that keep people fat, and a clear path to systematic weight loss.

ABOUT THE AUTHOR

Jason Fung is a Toronto-based kidney specialist and author. He is the founder of the Intensive Dietary Management Program in Toronto, which provides treatment for obesity and type 2 diabetes. Fung has been practicing at Scarborough General Hospital since 2001. He has coauthored a fasting guide with Jimmy Moore.

THE END

If you enjoyed this summary, please leave an honest review on Amazon.com…it'd mean a lot to us.

If you haven't already, we encourage you to purchase a copy of the original book.

Made in the USA
San Bernardino, CA
29 April 2019